Cornerstones of Freedom

The Thirteen Colonies

GAIL SAKURAI

CHILDREN'S PRESS®
A Division of Grolier Publishing
New York • London • Hong Kong • Sydney
Danbury, Connecticut

Missionaries meeting with American Indians

Visit Children's Press on the Internet at:
http://publishing.grolier.com

Library of Congress Cataloging-in-Publication Data

Sakurai, Gail.
The Thirteen Colonies / Gail Sakurai.
    p. cm.—(Cornerstones of freedom)
    Includes index.
    Summary: Describes the history of the thirteen original English colonies
in America, including their early exploration, settlement, and regional
differences.
    ISBN: 0-516-21603-1 (lib. bdg.)   0-516-27091-5 (pbk.)
1. United States—History—Colonial period, ca. 1600–1775—Juvenile literature.
[1. United States—History—Colonial period, ca. 1600–1775.] I. Title. II. Series.
E188.S17   2000
973.2—dc 21
                                              99-053533
                                                   CIP
                                                    AC

©2000 Children's Press®
A Division of Grolier Publishing Co., Inc.
All rights reserved. Published simultaneously in Canada.
Printed in the United States of America.
1 2 3 4 5 6 7 8 9 10 R 09 08 07 06 05 04 03 02 01 00

In the years following Christopher Columbus's first voyage to the New World in 1492, daring sea captains from several European nations explored the eastern coast of America in small wooden sailing ships. At first, Europeans visited North America only to explore the region and fish in the waters off the coast. Later, Spain, France, England, and the Netherlands all claimed parts of North America as a result of these explorations. Each of these European countries wanted to enlarge its empire by claiming the most land and acquiring the most wealth.

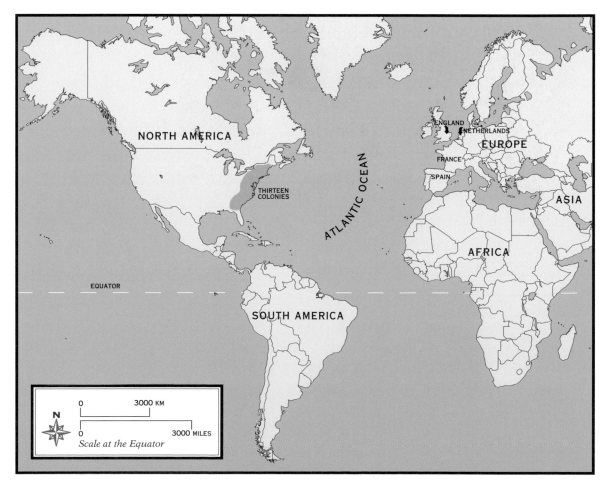

Spanish explorers came searching for gold and other riches, which they found in present-day Mexico and South America. Spain also sent missionaries who wanted to convert the American Indians to Christianity. It was the first country to establish a colony in what is now the United States. In 1565, the Spanish founded Saint Augustine in present-day Florida.

France sent explorers and missionaries to North America, too, but the French wanted furs rather than gold. The French fur traders established trading posts and small forts. They traded tools, blankets, and other items to the Indians, in exchange for thick furs that were popular in Europe.

England claimed a large tract of land along the east coast of North America, between French Canada to the north and Spanish Florida to the south. The English called this new land Virginia. The first English attempt to establish a colony in Virginia came in 1585. Sir Walter Raleigh sent a group of 108 men to Roanoke Island off the coast of what is now North Carolina. The settlers found the conditions there so harsh and forbidding that they returned to England the following year.

Raleigh sent a second group of 117 colonists to Virginia in 1587. John White led the 91 men, 17 women, and 9 children. On August 18, 1587, just a few days after arriving at Roanoke Island,

John White's daughter, Eleanor Dare, gave birth to a baby girl. She named the baby Virginia, after the new land. Virginia Dare was the first child of English-speaking parents in North America.

John White helped the colonists get settled in their new land. At the end of August 1587, he sailed back to England for supplies, leaving his family behind on Roanoke. Soon afterward, war broke out between England and Spain, preventing White from returning to America. When he was finally able to return in August 1590, he found the colony abandoned.

The only clue to the settlers' whereabouts was the word "Croatoan" carved on a tree. The Croatoan Indians were friendly people who lived on an island south of Roanoke. White thought that perhaps the colonists had gone to seek shelter with the Croatoans. Unfortunately, bad weather forced White to give up his search for the settlers, and he returned to England. He never saw his family again. The fate of the Roanoke colonists remains a mystery. As a result, the settlement is known as the Lost Colony.

Sir Walter Raleigh sent settlers to establish a colony in North America.

England waited nearly seventeen years before trying to establish another American colony. In May 1607, a group of 144 men and boys sailed to Virginia, where they established the first permanent English colony in America. They built a fort and a small town on a peninsula in the middle of the James River. The colonists called their settlement Jamestown.

The first Jamestown colonists were adventurers who hoped to quickly make a fortune in the New World and then return

Modern replicas of the Susan Constant, Godspeed, *and* Discovery, *the three ships that arrived in Jamestown in May 1607.*

to England as wealthy men. Most of them were not used to hard work. They did not have the skills needed to survive in the wilderness. They argued among themselves and wasted their time looking for gold and silver instead of planting crops and hunting for food. Before long, many settlers became ill and weak from lack of food and clean drinking water. By the end of that first summer, more than half the colonists had died. Captain John Smith, one of Jamestown's leaders, traded with the local Indians for some corn to tide the settlers over until fresh supplies arrived from England.

The little colony continued to struggle for survival. The lowest point came during the winter of 1609–10. So many people died during that winter that the colonists called it "the starving time." Pocahontas, daughter of the Indian chief Powhatan, befriended the settlers. The corn she brought them during those months saved many starving colonists from death. Nevertheless, by spring the settlers were ready to abandon the colony and return to England. The colony was finally saved when a new governor, Lord De la Warr, arrived with more settlers and fresh supplies.

Captain John Smith

Growing tobacco at Colonial Williamsburg

Around 1612, the Jamestown settlers began successfully growing tobacco, a valuable crop that sold for high prices in Europe. The colonists had discovered that the soil and climate in Virginia were particularly well-suited for tobacco cultivation. Tobacco sold well and provided new opportunities for farmers and merchants. Jamestown and the Virginia Colony grew rapidly and prospered. Hundreds of new settlers arrived from England each year. The colony spread out, and new towns were built all over Virginia. Large tobacco farms, called plantations, were started to meet Europe's increasing demand for Virginia tobacco.

As the colony expanded and the tobacco industry grew, the demand for cheap labor grew, too. The colonists turned to indentured servants and slaves to fill their need for more workers. Indentured servants were usually people who wanted to come to America but couldn't afford to pay the fare for the ocean voyage. Indentured servants agreed to work without pay for a specific period of time, usually from four to seven years. In return, the servants received a place on a boat to America, food, clothing, and shelter during their service. Sometimes indentured servants were given money, tools, or land at the end of their service to help them get started in their new life. Many poor English people and other Europeans came to America in this way. The first Africans who arrived in Jamestown in 1619 were brought as indentured servants.

While indentured servants entered into service willingly and eventually gained their freedom, slaves were taken from their homes in western Africa and brought to America against their will, with no hope of eventual freedom. Some slaves worked as house servants or craftsmen, but most were forced into backbreaking labor on tobacco plantations. Growing tobacco required many laborers. All the planting, hoeing, trimming, drying, and other work involved in growing tobacco had to be done by hand. As the demand for tobacco grew, slavery increased. Gradually, slaves replaced indentured servants as a source of cheap labor.

An early group of African slaves arrives in Jamestown.

In 1619, the year the first Africans arrived in Jamestown, two other important events occured in the Virginia Colony. Women arrived from England, offering the colony's men companionship and a chance to marry and start families. Also, Jamestown's leaders created an elected assembly, the first representative legislature in the North America. This assembly satisfied the colonists' demands for a greater voice in their government.

Although the first Jamestown colonists came to America seeking a fortune, the second group of English people came to the colonies looking for religious freedom. In England, the Church of England was the official church and no other religions were permitted. People who disagreed with the Church of England or belonged to other religious groups were often imprisoned, exiled, or even executed. People who wanted to separate from the Church of England and set up their own church were called Separatists.

One group of Separatists left England to escape persecution. They called themselves Pilgrims, which means "homeless wanderers." The Pilgrims and their families lived in the Netherlands for a number of years, but the parents were worried. They were afraid that the children would forget their English heritage and grow up speaking Dutch instead of English. They finally decided to make a new home in

America. In the colonies, they could live as English citizens but would be able to worship according to their own beliefs, far away from the interference of the Church of England.

The Pilgrims convinced some English merchants to provide transportation and supplies for their group. In return, the colonists agreed to send back valuable goods for the merchants to sell in England. The merchants recruited 61 people to join the 41 Pilgrims on their voyage and help them establish a new colony in America. The Pilgrims called the other travelers Strangers.

The Pilgrims and Strangers left England in September 1620 aboard a small wooden sailing ship called the *Mayflower*. The ocean crossing lasted more than two stormy months. Many of the travelers were ill and suffered greatly from the poor food and rough weather. They finally reached Cape Cod in November 1620.

The Mayflower *approaching the coast of Massachusetts in 1620*

Before setting foot on their new land, the colonists held a meeting aboard ship and adopted a plan for governing their colony. Everyone, Pilgrim and Stranger alike, agreed to make laws that were fair and to live together in peace and harmony with equal rights for all. They called their agreement the Mayflower Compact.

For several weeks, small groups went ashore to look for a good site for their settlement, while the rest of the colonists remained on board the ship. Finally, a location was chosen on the west side of Cape Cod Bay in what is now Massachusetts. The colonists called their new home Plymouth, after a port city in England.

Their first winter in the new land was long and cold, and many of the Plymouth colonists died of hunger and disease. Only half of the original colonists were still alive by spring 1621. One spring day, Samoset, a leader of the nearby Pemaquid tribe, walked into Plymouth. He welcomed the colonists and offered them friendship. The colonists were startled to hear him speaking English, which he had learned from English explorers and fishermen. Later, Samoset returned with Squanto, a Patuxet Indian who had lived in England for several years and spoke more English than Samoset did. Squanto taught the colonists how to plant corn, pumpkins, and beans and showed them the best places to hunt and fish.

Samoset and Squanto introduced the Plymouth colonists to Massasoit, the great chief of the Wampanoag tribe. The colonists and Massasoit agreed to a treaty of peace and friendship, which remained in effect for fifty years.

That fall, after a good harvest, the Plymouth colonists decided to hold a feast to celebrate the harvest and to thank God for their survival. They invited their American Indian friends to share the festival with them. The colonists provided ducks, geese, turkeys, clams, fish, corn bread, and a variety of vegetables. Ninety Indians attended and brought five deer to add to the meal, which everyone ate outdoors at large tables. That celebration, which lasted for three days, has become known as the first Thanksgiving.

The first Thanksgiving

People visit this modern re-creation of Plimoth Plantation in Plymouth, Massachusetts.

The Plymouth Colony continued to prosper and grow. Its success encouraged others who were seeking religious freedom and new land to settle in America. Earlier, Captain John Smith had explored the coast of present-day New Hampshire and had written about it. A few years after the Pilgrims arrived, colonists settled in New Hampshire. A Scotsman, David Thomson, founded what is now the town of Rye in 1623. New Hampshire became the third colony settled after Virginia and Massachusetts.

Many Puritans founded settlements in the Massachusetts Bay area, including the town of Boston in 1630. Puritans were English people who wished to reform the Church of England and simplify its ceremonies and rituals. Although Puritans wanted religious freedom for themselves, they were not willing to give other people in their colonies the same liberty.

They strongly believed that it was best for the community if everyone shared the same religious beliefs. As a result, they frequently punished or expelled people who dared to disagree with their Puritan beliefs.

Other settlements sprang up all around the Massachusetts Bay area in the 1630s. People heard about the rich farmland in what is now Connecticut, and many settled there. Thomas Hooker, a Puritan, was the chief founder of Hartford, Connecticut. In 1636, Hartford, Wethersfield, and Windsor united to form the Connecticut Colony.

Puritans shaped religion, social life, and government in North America.

Nearby Rhode Island was settled by religious exiles from Massachusetts. Roger Williams, a Massachusetts minister, was expelled by the Puritans because he called for increased religious and political freedom. Williams was driven out of the colony in the dead of winter. He was forced to live off the land for over three months, sleeping in hollow trees and eating acorns, roots, and parched corn to survive. In 1636, Williams and his followers founded the town of Providence, the first English settlement in Rhode Island.

Anne Hutchinson was put on trial for her religious beliefs and later banned from Boston.

Anne Hutchinson angered the Puritans by claiming the right to speak at worship services. At that time, women had no legal rights and were supposed to keep silent in church. Puritan leaders believed that, "women have no business at these assemblies. . . ." Hutchinson and her followers were banished from Massachusetts. In 1638, they went to Rhode Island, where Roger Williams welcomed them.

Puritans valued education highly. They established Harvard College, the first institution of higher education in America, in 1636. Wealthy families could hire a private tutor to teach their children. They also had the option of sending their children to private schools in the colonies or in England. Puritans wanted all their children to be able to read the Bible for themselves. In 1647, the Massachusetts Colony set up the first public school system in

Harvard College in the 1740s

America. The law required every town with at least fifty families to start an elementary school for all children. In addition, any town with one hundred or more families had to set up a secondary school, called a Latin grammar school, to prepare boys for college.

Because paper was scarce and expensive in the early colonies, children didn't study from real books. Instead, they used hornbooks to study their lessons. A hornbook was a flat board with a handle. The lesson was written on a piece of paper and pasted to the wood. Then a thin, flat piece of animal horn was fastened over the paper to protect it. The horn was clear so that the lesson could be read through it. Lessons generally included the alphabet, numbers, a Bible verse, and the Lord's Prayer. Often, a cord or string was looped through a hole in the handle of the hornbook, so that students could wear them around their necks.

Some young people learned a trade by serving as apprentices. Under the apprenticeship system, a boy's parents could place him with a master craftsman or tradesman, such as a blacksmith or a merchant. The master would teach his skills to the boy and provide him with food, clothing, and lodging. In return, the boy promised to work hard and be obedient. As the apprentice learned and his skill increased, he would be given more interesting duties and greater responsibility.

England wasn't the only nation to establish North American colonies between French Canada and Spanish Florida. In 1624, about thirty Dutch families from the Netherlands settled along the Hudson River in what is now New York. They called their colony New Netherland. The following year, a group of Dutch colonists began building a town named New Amsterdam on the southern tip of Manhattan Island. Peter Minuit, the Dutch governor, bought Manhattan from the local Indians for goods worth sixty Dutch guilders, or about twenty-four dollars.

In 1638, people from Sweden founded the colony of New Sweden in the area that would later become the colonies of Delaware (named after Lord De la Warr), and New Jersey (named after England's Isle of Jersey). The colonists called their settlement Fort Christina, after

Peter Minuit purchased Manhattan Island from the local Indians.

the eleven-year-old queen of Sweden. In 1642, Swedish colonists along the Delaware River built the first log cabins in the New World. The walls were made of logs fitted together, and the cracks between the logs were filled with mud and moss. Log cabins became a popular form of housing on the frontier. By 1655, about 350 people were living in New Sweden when Dutch troops captured it and made it part of New Netherland.

War broke out between England and the Netherlands in 1664. English soldiers under the leadership of the Duke of York captured all the Dutch colonies in America without firing a single shot. After the Dutch surrender, the area was renamed New York, in honor of the Duke of York.

In 1681, King Charles II of England granted a large region of land in America to William Penn, in payment of a debt that the king owed to Penn's deceased father. The new colony was named Pennsylvania, which means "Penn's Woodlands." William Penn was a member of the Religious Society of Friends, commonly called Quakers. Like the Pilgrims, the Quakers were a religious group that disagreed with the

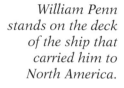

William Penn stands on the deck of the ship that carried him to North America.

Church of England. Quakers believe that all people are equal, regardless of race, color, or religion. They insist on equality for women and allow women to speak and preach. Penn wanted his colony to offer complete religious freedom and equality for all. While Penn was in charge, many American Indians came to Pennsylvania because there they could live in peace.

Penn drew up a plan of government for his colony and began laying out the streets for Philadelphia, the colony's main settlement. By 1685, eight thousand Quakers had come to Pennsylvania. Philadelphia quickly became the largest and most prosperous city in the English colonies.

Philadelphia in the 1730s

Sir George Calvert founded the colony of Maryland as a religious refuge for Roman Catholics, who were also persecuted in England. The first group of two hundred settlers, including two Catholic priests, arrived in Maryland in March 1634, on two ships called the *Ark* and the *Dove*. In 1649, Maryland passed the first religious toleration act in the colonies, granting religious freedom to all Christians.

Settlers spreading out from Virginia founded North Carolina around 1650. This colony often experienced conflict, including revolts against its governors. Between 1664 and 1689, the colony had five governors. Pirates, such as the villain known as Blackbeard, terrorized the settlers. In addition, colonists often had to battle the wilderness and the American Indians.

Edward Teach, known as Blackbeard

European settlement also moved southward. In 1670, colonists landed in present-day South Carolina. Later, rice and indigo were grown there on large plantations that used slave labor. Indigo was a West Indies plant that was prized for its rich blue dye. In 1739, sixteen-year-old Eliza Lucas began experimenting with growing indigo in South Carolina. After four years of work, she developed a variety of indigo plant that could survive the hot and humid South Carolina summers. Thanks to her work, indigo became an important crop in the colonies.

Georgia was the last of the colonies to be established. It was founded by James Oglethorpe, who wanted to provide a safe place for British debtors. In Great Britain, poor people who could not pay their debts were often sent to prison. The first group of 120 colonists arrived in Georgia in early 1733 and founded the town of Savannah.

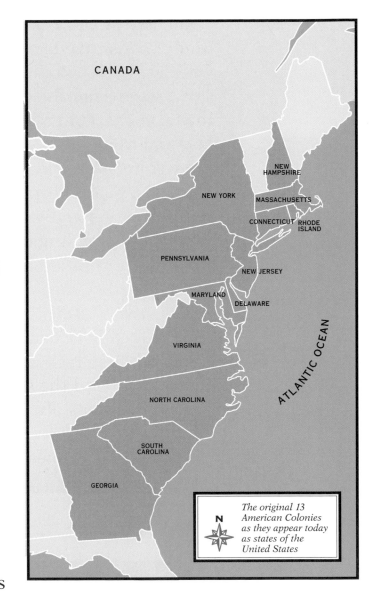

The original 13 American Colonies as they appear today as states of the United States

By 1740, there were thirteen English colonies in North America, with a total population of 700,000. The thirteen colonies were: Virginia, Massachusetts, New Hampshire, New York, Connecticut, Maryland, Rhode Island, Delaware, Pennsylvania, North Carolina, New Jersey, South Carolina, and Georgia.

The early colonists struggled and overcame many hardships to create a new home in the wilderness. Most colonists were farmers, but some were fishermen and others found jobs in towns as craftsmen and merchants. The typical colonial family lived on a small farm, where they grew corn, beans, and squash. They also raised chickens, pigs, sheep, and cows. Their house was made of wood and was heated by a large central fireplace that was also used for cooking. Colonial meals were simple but plentiful. Corn was a part of nearly every meal. The colonists ate corn bread, corn pudding, fresh roasted ears of corn, and many other corn dishes. The family's cow provided fresh milk and cream, and each family

A farmer feeding his pigs in the early 1600s

made its own butter and cheese. In addition to milk, they drank cider, beer, wine, and rum. Clothing was made at home by hand, as was their sturdy heavy wooden furniture. Children often did the same work as the adults, working alongside their parents. Boys helped their fathers with the planting and harvesting, while girls helped their mothers prepare meals and make clothing.

At first, travel in colonial America was mostly on foot or by boat on rivers or streams. There were no roads, only ancient Indian trails through the forests. Eventually, as towns and cities grew, dirt roads were built. The Boston Post Road, connecting the cities of Boston and New York, was completed in 1672. Today, the same road is a paved highway carrying cars and trucks.

There was no real postal service in the early colonies. The only way to send a letter was to ask a friend or neighbor who was traveling in the right direction to deliver it. The traveler usually dropped the letter at a tavern or shop in the nearest town, and days or even weeks might pass before the letter was picked up. In 1753, Benjamin Franklin of Pennsylvania and William Hunter of Virginia were appointed to manage the colonial postal service. They established post offices in all the colonies and improved mail delivery service.

Benjamin Franklin

As the colonies grew and settlements spread out, the American Indians suffered. Many Indians died of the diseases brought to North America by Europeans. Indians were driven out of their ancient lands and pushed farther and farther west by the land-hungry colonists. Some tribes struggled to live in harmony with the newcomers, but others fought bitter wars against them.

War affected the lives of most people in the colonies. When British colonists started settling the lands west of the Appalachian Mountains,

French and English forces fighting during the French and Indian War

they ran into opposition from the French. France claimed the area between the Appalachians and the Mississippi River as its own territory. Some American Indian tribes sided with the British in this dispute, while other tribes allied themselves with the French. The struggle between the two countries turned into a long series of four wars called the French and Indian Wars. The last of the four wars began in 1754 and finally ended with a British victory in 1763. As a result, the French lost most of their territory in North America to Great Britain.

Although it won the French and Indian Wars, the fight had been long and expensive, and Great Britain was deeply in debt. The British government decided to tax the American colonies to raise funds. Britain placed taxes on various goods brought into the colonies, including molasses, glass, lead, paint, paper, and tea. Many Americans resented these taxes. The colonists wanted to govern themselves without interference from Britain. They believed that only their own elected colonial assemblies had the right to tax them. Each time a new tax was imposed, the Americans responded angrily. Colonial leaders organized public protests against the taxes and urged the colonists to boycott all British goods. American protests led Great Britain to impose even more taxes and restrictions.

As the years passed, the American colonists became increasingly upset with British rule, and violent public resistance grew. By 1775, war had broken out between the colonies and Great Britain. Many colonists believed that the only solution to the conflict was independence from Britain. On July 4, 1776, representatives from the thirteen original colonies issued the Declaration of Independence, and the colonial era came to an end. The Declaration listed the reasons for separating from Great Britain. It proclaimed that all people were entitled to "life, liberty, and the pursuit of happiness." Most important, the document announced the formation of a new nation, the United States of America.

Left: Minutemen march to fight in the American Revolution. Right: The Declaration of Independence is among the most treasured documents in U.S. history.

FUN FACTS ABOUT LIFE IN THE THIRTEEN COLONIES

• Instead of eating their main meal in the evening, most colonists ate dinner between noon and three o'clock.

• Milk and water were not popular drinks in colonial days, but apple cider was. Colonial children drank cider as often as some children drink soft drinks today.

• Most Puritan congregations had seating arrangements. Each seat was assigned according to the person's social rank, including age, family, wealth, and service to the community.

• In 1650, there were about 50,000 people from Europe living in the English colonies. Fifty years later, that number had increased by five times, to about 125,000. By 1750, that number had increased again by five times, to about 1,250,000, including 240,000 Africans.

• The first book written and printed for children in the American colonies was John Cotton's religious book, *Spiritual Milk for Boston Babes in Either England, Drawn from the Breasts of Both Testaments for Their Souls' Nourishment* (1656).

• Today, kids still play some of the games that were popular among children in the thirteen colonies: blindman's bluff, hide-and-seek, hopscotch, leapfrog, and tag.

• The colonists had to develop new words for the objects and experiences that they had in their new land. Some of the English words that date back to colonial times include: *canoe, toboggan, raccoon, skunk, groundhog, squash, pecan, snow plow, sleigh, foothill,* and *prairie.*

GLOSSARY

apprentice – a person who learns a trade or business by working with someone who is skilled in that field

blacksmith – a person who repairs or makes objects from iron

boycott – to refuse to use or buy certain goods as a protest

colony – a territory that is far away from the country that governs it

colonies

cultivate – to prepare soil for the planting and raising of crops

debt – something that is owed to another person

empire – a group of countries under one government or ruler

frontier – the far edge of a country, where few people live

indigo – a plant used to make a blue dye; grown in warm climates

legislature – a group of people who make laws for a colony, state, or country

merchant – a person who buys and sells goods; a shopkeeper or trader

port

peninsula – a body of land surrounded on three sides by water

persecute – to cause great suffering, especially because of political beliefs, religion, or race

plantation – a large farm in the southern colonies

port – a city with a harbor where large ships can anchor

refuge – protection or shelter from danger or trouble

slavery – a system in which people own other people

TIMELINE

Christopher Columbus **1492**
discovers the New World

Spain founds St. Augustine, the first **1565**
colony in North America

1585 .... First English attempt to begin
Lost Colony founded **1587** a colony at Roanoke Island

1607 Jamestown Colony founded

First legislature in North America **1619**
meets at Jamestown; first Africans **1620** Pilgrims found Plymouth Colony
and women arrive in Jamestown **1623** New Hampshire founded
1624 Dutch found New Netherland

1634 Catholics found Maryland

Roger Williams founds Providence, ... **1636**
Rhode Island; three settlements **1638** New Sweden founded
form the Connecticut Colony

1650 North Carolina founded

Colonists land in South Carolina **1670**

1681 Quakers found Pennsylvania

Georgia Colony founded **1733**

1754

1763

1775
July 4: Declaration of **1776** American Revolutionary War
Last French and Independence signed
Indian War **1783**

INDEX (*Boldface* page numbers indicate illustrations.)

PHOTO CREDITS

Photographs ©: Brown Brothers: 2; Connecticut Historical Society: 24; Corbis-Bettmann: 28 left, 31 bottom right (Col. Louis Frohman), cover, 5, 9, 11, 13, 15, 16, 19, 20, 21, 25, 30, 31 top; H. Armstrong Roberts, Inc.: 14 (J. Blank), 6 (D. Campione); N.C. Department of Cultural Resources Div. of Archives & History: 22; New York Public Library Picture Collection: 17; North Wind Picture Archives: 1, 7, 8, 26, 31 bottom left; Stock Montage, Inc.: 12; Superstock, Inc.: 28 right.
Maps by TJS Design, Inc.

PICTURE IDENTIFICATIONS

Cover photo: A colonial common room
Page 1: Helpful American Indians taught the New England colonists about the region.

ABOUT THE AUTHOR

Gail Sakurai is a children's author who specializes in retelling folk tales and writing nonfiction for young readers. *The Thirteen Colonies* is her tenth book. Ms. Sakurai lives in Cincinnati, Ohio, with her husband and two sons. When she is not researching or writing, she enjoys traveling with her family and visiting America's historical sites.